Contents

Grammar

Punctuation

Why do we need grammar and punctuation?

Grammar and punctuation are very important tools. They help you organize your words so their meaning is clear, and they make your writing much easier to read.

Writing without punctuation is very hard to read.

understand I don't.

Words that don't follow the rules of grammar can be extremely confusing.

weve lost pip our dog with a patch over one eye and a curly tail hes very friendly have you seen him anywhere we wonder if so please contact us

What is grammar anyway?

Grammar is a set of rules for using words. Each word in a sentence has a job to do and there are clear guidelines for how words work together.

Grammar is very helpful.

These words follow the rules of grammar.

Usborne

First Illustrated Grammar and Punctuation

Jane Bingham

Illustrated by Jordan Wray

Designed by
Stephanie Jeffries and Kirsty Tizzard

Consultant: John Seely
Edited by Felicity Brooks

Usborne Quicklinks

There are really good websites about grammar and punctuation, where children can watch animated explanations, test their understanding with online puzzles and quizzes, and build their writing skills with printable activities and exercises. We have selected a wide variety of these websites and provided links to them from the Usborne Quicklinks website.

To visit the recommended websites, go to the Usborne Quicklinks website at **www.usborne.com/quicklinks** and enter the keywords **first grammar and punctuation**.

Online safety

We recommend that young children are supervised while using the internet and that they follow the online safety guidelines displayed on the Usborne Quicklinks website. You'll also find more tips and advice for keeping children safe online on the website.

And what is punctuation?

Punctuation is the name for a set of signs, such as full stops and question marks. Punctuation marks divide words into groups and act as signposts, making writing easier to follow.

We have lost Pip.

Have you seen him?

Please contact us!

These punctuation marks help to make the meaning clear.

Watch your writing!

Grammar and punctuation are especially important when you write something such as instructions. Because you won't be there to explain, the meaning of your words must be clear to your reader.

These instructions are so easy to follow!

They tell us exactly what we need to do.

How this book works

This easy-to-use guide introduces you to the rules of grammar and punctuation. You can choose a topic to learn about or you can work your way through the book.

Clear headings introduce each topic.

Word lists provide useful examples.

Key words and phrases are underlined.

Rules are explained in simple, friendly language.

Yes! Now I understand!

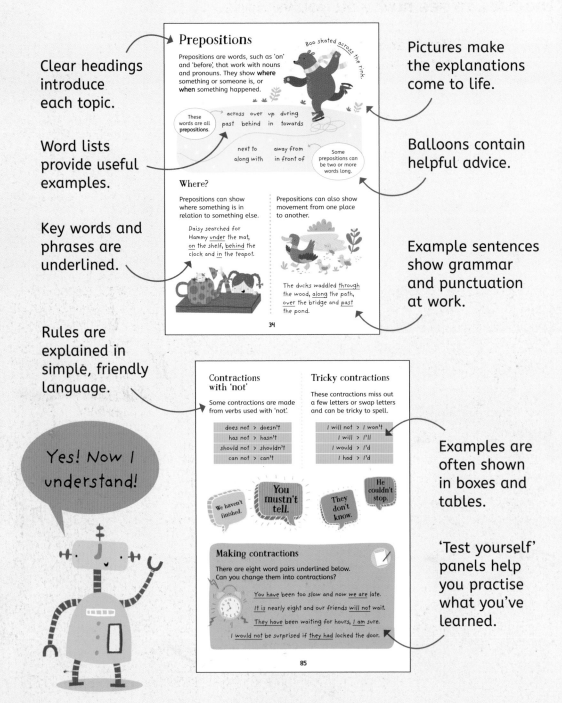

Pictures make the explanations come to life.

Balloons contain helpful advice.

Example sentences show grammar and punctuation at work.

Examples are often shown in boxes and tables.

'Test yourself' panels help you practise what you've learned.

Quizzes to test yourself

There are quizzes at every stage to help you test your knowledge. Use a pen and paper for your answers. Then, turn to the back of the book to see how well you've done.

Hooray! I got it right!

Here's an example of a quiz. Look out for this sign to test yourself.

Example quiz

Can you find six main clauses and three linking words?

Do you like dogs, or do you prefer cats? Dogs are very friendly, but they need a lot of exercise. I take Dilly to the park and I often play outside with her.

Improve your writing

Would you like to be a better writer? Look at pages 90 to 93 to learn about **writing skills** and find out ways to make your writing more exciting.

haunted

mysterious

shadowy

rustling

ghostly

eerie

The Enchanted Forest

Word classes

Each time you speak or write, you put together a mixture of different kinds of words, known as **word classes**. Each word class has its own particular job to do.

Nouns tell you the name of a person, an animal, a thing or a place.

> Joe   tiger   shop   Rome

Adverbs tell you more about the way something is done.

> loudly   soon   carefully

Pronouns can stand for a noun.

> I   you   it
> she   they

Prepositions show the position of something, or when something happened.

> under   through   during

Adjectives tell you more about someone or something.

> pink   huge   exciting

Conjunctions make a link between different parts of a sentence.

> and   but   or   because

Verbs are 'doing', 'thinking' or 'being' words.

> swim   imagine   be   have

Articles* go in front of a noun to make it clearer what you're talking about.

> the   a   an

*Articles belong to a larger word class, called **determiners**.

You don't often see all the word classes together, but the sentence below contains them all:

Katy	noun
and	conjunction
I	pronoun
swam	verb
slowly	adverb
around	preposition
the	article
crumbling	adjective
wreck.	noun

Nouns

Nouns are words that tell you the name of something. A noun can be a person, an animal, a thing or a place.

Molly   walrus   computer   India

magic   clouds   castle   helicopter

Proper nouns

A proper noun tells you the name of one particular person, place or thing.

For example, 'London' is a proper noun because it's a particular place.

I love London

Proper nouns start with a capital letter.

Freddie
Japan
Mars
Professor Pink
Wednesday
Texas

Proper nouns include...

• people's names

Lauren
Archibald
Dr Brown

• places, countries, continents

Tokyo
Australia
Asia

• days, months, festivals

Saturday
August
Christmas
Diwali

Common nouns

You use a common noun when you're <u>not</u> talking about a particular person, place or thing.

So, 'rabbit' is a common noun because there can be lots of rabbits.

Common nouns don't have a capital letter unless they are the first word in a sentence.

cake
hat
star
kitten
table

Abstract nouns

Some nouns name a thing that can't be seen, heard, touched, smelled or tasted. They are called abstract nouns.

love
beauty
education
happiness
peace

Abstract nouns are common nouns, so they don't have a capital letter.

Spot the nouns

Can you spot seven nouns in this sentence?

Eva had a dream that she saw an elephant with purple spots riding a bicycle through the parks of Paris.

More about nouns

Singular and plural

A noun can be singular and stand for just one thing, or it can be plural and stand for more than one thing.

'dog' is a **singular** noun.

'dogs' is a **plural** noun.

Making plurals

Most nouns change their spelling when they become plural.

hat	>	hat**s**
girl	>	girl**s**
ferry	>	ferr**ies**
fox	>	fox**es**

Add 'es'

If a noun ends in **s**, **ss**, **x**, **ch** or **sh**, you need to add **es**.

bus	>	bus**es**
dress	>	dress**es**
box	>	box**es**
watch	>	watch**es**

Just add 's'

To make a noun plural, you usually just add a letter **s**.

diamond	>	diamond**s**
bicycle	>	bicycle**s**
shoe	>	shoe**s**

brush   brush**es**

You also add **es** to most nouns ending in **o**.

hero	>	her**oes**
potato	>	potat**oes**

Vowels and consonants

The five **vowels** are:

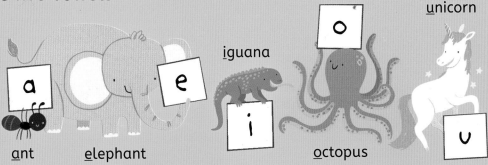

ant elephant iguana octopus unicorn

a e i o u

The **consonants** are all the other letters of the alphabet:

a b c d e f g h i j k l m n o p q r s t u v w x y z

Watch out for 'y'!

If a noun ends in a vowel plus **y**, just add a letter **s**.

boy	>	boy_s_
key	>	key_s_
day	>	day_s_

If a noun ends in a consonant plus **y**, change the **y** to **i** and add **es**.

baby	>	bab_ies_
story	>	stor_ies_
fly	>	fl_ies_

Watch out for 'f'!

If a noun ends in **f** or **fe**, you often need to change the **f** or **fe** to **ves**.

elf	>	el_ves_
half	>	hal_ves_
knife	>	kni_ves_

leaf

leaves

More about nouns

Unusual plurals

Some nouns change in an unusual way when they become plural.

woman	>	women
man	>	men
child	>	children
mouse	>	mice

goose > geese

> Nouns that change in an unusual way are called **irregular nouns**.

No change

A few nouns stay exactly the same in their singular and plural forms.

sheep	>	sheep
deer	>	deer
series	>	series
fish	>	fish

aircraft > aircraft

No singular

These nouns are always plural:

clothes   jeans   sunglasses

trousers   pants   goggles

scissors

Compound nouns

Compound nouns are made by putting two or more words together.

Some are written as a single word:

whiteboard
playgroup
motorbike
toyshop

Some are two or more separate words:

ice cream
bus stop
merry-go-round
swimming pool

Plural compound nouns

The usual way to make a plural compound noun is to add a letter **s** to the final word.

toyshop<u>s</u>
swimming poo<u>ls</u>
merry-go-round<u>s</u>

motorbike<u>s</u>

Compound nouns can be tricky to spell, so it's a good idea to check your spelling in a dictionary.

Singular to plural

Can you change these singular nouns into plural nouns?

top hat   monkey   thief   lunch

mouse   fairy   kiss   tomato

Pronouns

Pronouns are little words, such as 'he' or 'us', that can take the place of a person, an animal or a thing.

I   you   she   it   him   we   them

Using pronouns

A pronoun can stand for a singular noun or a plural noun.

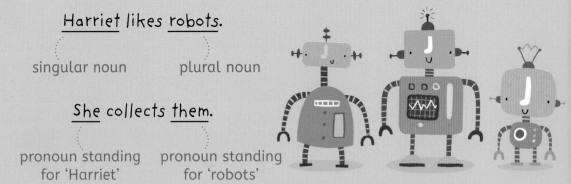

Harriet likes robots.

singular noun   plural noun

She collects them.

pronoun standing   pronoun standing
for 'Harriet'   for 'robots'

Spot the pronouns

There are seven pronouns in this message. Can you find them all?

Dad is taking us with him to see the castle. He says it is amazing. We are going tomorrow. I hope you can come.

Why use pronouns?

When you use pronouns in your writing, you don't have to write the same words over and over again.

So, instead of this...

> George loves bananas. George eats bananas every day. Bananas make George feel happy.

you can write this...

pronoun

> George loves bananas. He eats them every day. They make him feel happy.

pronouns

These sentences sound better and they're shorter, too!

Which pronoun?

Look at the story below. Can you use a pronoun to replace the words that are underlined? Choose from the pronouns in the orange panel.

> Sam and Tam went for a walk. On the way home, Sam and Tam saw Meg. Meg showed Sam and Tam a butterfly. The butterfly was beautiful.

She   they   It   them

Adjectives

Adjectives are describing words, such as 'funny' or 'short'. They tell you more about someone or something.

stripy

spotty

tall   noisy   unusual   hungry

difficult   magnificent   furry   surprising

Describing things

Adjectives give you information about a noun or a pronoun.

Ed has a new kite.

adjective   noun

It is colourful.

pronoun   adjective

You can use more than one adjective to describe something.

Ed has a beautiful new kite.

adjectives

It is large and colourful.

Spot the adjectives

Can you spot seven adjectives in this description?

The weather was calm and sunny as we sailed across the sparkling ocean. We felt proud and contented in our small green boat.

Adjectives for comparisons

You can use adjectives to compare people or things. Adjectives used in comparisons are called **comparatives** and **superlatives**.

The yacht is <u>big</u>.

adjective

The fishing boat is <u>bigger</u>.

comparative

The cruise ship is <u>the biggest</u>.

superlative

You use a comparative to compare **two** people or things.

You use a superlative to compare **three or more** people or things.

Making comparatives and superlatives

To make a comparative, add **er** to the end of an adjective.

long	>	long<u>er</u>
small	>	small<u>er</u>
slow	>	slow<u>er</u>

To make a superlative, add **est** to an adjective and put the word **the** in front of it.

long	>	<u>the longest</u>
small	>	<u>the smallest</u>
slow	>	<u>the slowest</u>

<u>the shortest</u>

More about adjectives

More comparatives and superlatives

If an adjective ends in **e**, add **r** to make the **comparative** and **st** to make the **superlative**.

> large > larg**er** > larg**est**
> fine > fin**er** > fin**est**

For some adjectives, you need to **double the last letter** before you add **er** or **est**.

> hot > ho**tter** > ho**ttest**
> sad > sa**dder** > sa**ddest**

wise   wis**er**   wis**est**

For adjectives that end in **y**, change the **y** to **i** before adding **er** or **est**.

> tidy > tid**ier** > tid**iest**
> happy > happ**ier** > happ**iest**

Good and bad

The adjectives 'good' and 'bad' don't follow the usual rules for forming comparatives and superlatives.

> good > better > best
> bad > worse > worst

Making comparisons

Can you complete these comparisons?

A cat is big___ than a mouse.

An elephant is heav___ than a horse.

More and the most

Long adjectives, such as 'wonderful', would sound very awkward if you added **er** or **est**. Instead, you need to say 'more wonderful' or 'the most wonderful'.

amazing

Add 'more' to make the **comparative**.

more amazing

the most amazing

Add 'the most' to make the **superlative**.

Using 'more' and 'the most'

You use 'more' and 'the most' when an adjective has **more than two syllables**. A syllable is a single sound, so the word 'amazing' has three syllables (a-maz-ing).

You need to use 'more' and 'the most' with all these adjectives.

beautiful

terrible

surprising

unusual

interesting

mysterious

Right or wrong?

Only one of these comparisons is correct. Can you spot it?

This is the beautifullest flower I have ever seen.
Cheese is more expensive than bread.
The test was difficulter than I expected.

Verbs

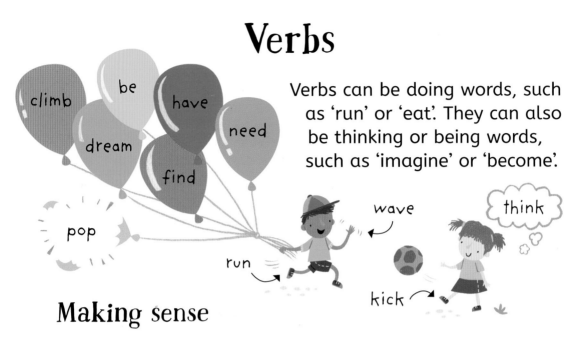

Verbs can be doing words, such as 'run' or 'eat'. They can also be thinking or being words, such as 'imagine' or 'become'.

Making sense

Every sentence needs at least one verb. If you take away the verb from a sentence, it will no longer make sense.

These three statements don't work without their verbs.

The lion roared.

Dan screamed loudly.

He ran as fast as the wind.

| The lion. | Dan loudly. | He as fast as the wind. |

Spot the verbs

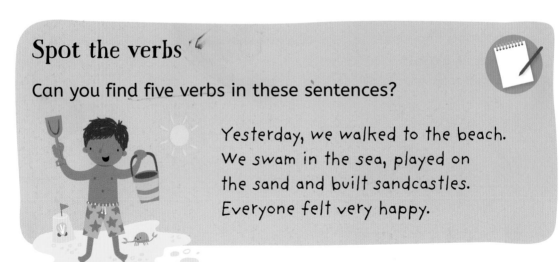

Can you find five verbs in these sentences?

Yesterday, we walked to the beach. We swam in the sea, played on the sand and built sandcastles. Everyone felt very happy.

22

Present and past

A verb can show an action in the **present** or the **past**. Here are some verb forms that show present and past actions.

Marina <u>combs</u> her hair every day.

> Verbs in the **simple present** show an action that often happens or usually happens.
>
> See page 24

Yesterday, she <u>combed</u> her hair fifty times.

> Verbs in the **simple past** show an action that happened and was completed in the past.
>
> See page 25

Marvin <u>is chasing</u> a fish.

> Verbs in the **present progressive** show an action that is happening now and continuing for a while.
>
> See page 27

He <u>was chasing</u> an octopus when he spotted Marina.

> Verbs in the **past progressive** show an action that started in the past and continued to another point in the past.
>
> See page 28

Marina <u>has discovered</u> an interesting shell.

> Verbs in the **present perfect** show an action that started in the past and is still important now.
>
> See page 29

More about verbs

Using the simple present

When a verb is used in the **simple present**, its spelling stays the same, except when the person doing the action is 'she', 'he' or 'it'.

Verbs in the **simple present** show an action that often happens or usually happens.

Adding 's'

If the person doing the action is 'she', 'he' or 'it', you need to add the letter **s** to most verbs.

She sings.　　He sings.　　It sings.

I sing
you sing
he sings
she sings
it sings
we sing
you sing
they sing

Add the letter **s**.

Adding 'es'

If a verb ends in **s**, **sh**, **ch**, **ss**, **z**, **zz**, or **x**, you need to add **es** when the person doing the action is 'she', 'he' or 'it'.

I splash	I mix
you splash	you mix
he/she/it splashes	he/she/it mixes
we splash	we mix
you splash	you mix
they splash	they mix

Add **es**.

Using the simple past

Verbs in the **simple past** show an action that happened and was completed in the past.

For most verbs, you form the **simple past** by adding **ed**.

work > work<u>ed</u>
look > look<u>ed</u>

For verbs that end in **e**, you just add **d**.

dance > danc<u>ed</u>
cycle > cycl<u>ed</u>
chase > chas<u>ed</u>

Some verbs **double their last letter** when you add **ed**. Here are some common examples:

stop > sto<u>pped</u>
plan > pla<u>nned</u>
spot > spo<u>tted</u>

Watch out for 'y'!

If a verb ends in a **vowel plus y**, you usually just add **ed** to form the simple past.

play > pla<u>yed</u>

He stayed and obeyed.

At least we tried.

If a verb ends in a **consonant plus y**, you change the **y** to **i** and add **ed**.

cry > cr<u>ied</u>
spy > sp<u>ied</u>
hurry > hurr<u>ied</u>

Turn back to page 13 to remind yourself about **vowels** and **consonants**.

More about verbs

'be' and 'have' – two very useful verbs

The verbs 'be' and 'have' don't follow the usual rules in their present and past forms:

simple present	simple past
I am	I was
you are	you were
he/she/it is	he/she/it was
we are	we were
you are	you were
they are	they were

be

simple present	simple past
I have	I had
you have	you had
he/she/it has	he/she/it had
we have	we had
you have	you had
they have	they had

have

Now, Caspar <u>is</u> huge.
Last year, he <u>was</u> tiny.
Now, he <u>has</u> long legs.
Then, he <u>had</u> short legs.

CASPAR

Using the present progressive

To form the **present progressive***, you use the verb 'be' as a helping verb** and add **ing** to the main verb.

Verbs in the **present progressive** show an action that is happening now and is continuing for a while.

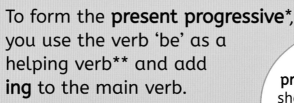

Hetty <u>is</u> <u>standing</u> on her hands.

helping verb   main verb

I <u>am</u> <u>reading</u> a book.

helping verb   ····· main verb

helping verb		main verb
I	am	growing
you	are	growing
he/she/it	is	growing
we	are	growing
you	are	growing
they	are	growing

Use the **simple present** of the verb 'be'.

Add **ing** to the main verb.

When you add **ing** to a verb, you make a **present participle**. Turn to page 30 to find out more.

*The present progressive is sometimes known as the **present continuous**.

27

Helping verbs are also known as **auxiliary verbs.

More about verbs

Using the past progressive

To form the **past progressive***, you use the simple past of the helping verb 'be' and add **ing** to the main verb.

Verbs in the **past progressive** show an action that started in the past and continued to another point in the past.

The sun <u>was</u> shining when we left home.

helping verb   main verb

We <u>were</u> playing before the rain started.

helping verb		main verb
I	was	looking
you	were	looking
he/she/it	was	looking
we	were	looking
you	were	looking
they	were	looking

Use the **simple past** of 'be'.

Add **ing** to the main verb.

Present progressive to past progressive

All the verbs below are in the present progressive. Can you change them to the past progressive?

I am dancing. You are skipping.
He is hopping. We are all having fun.

*The past progressive is sometimes known as the **past continuous**.

Using the present perfect

To form the **present perfect**, you use the simple present of the helping verb 'have' and add **ed** to the main verb.

Verbs in the **present perfect** show an action that started in the past and is still important now.

We <u>have</u> <u>walked</u> for miles.

helping verb ····· main verb

Yaz <u>has</u> <u>spotted</u> a signpost.

helping verb ····· main verb

helping verb		main verb
I	have	jumped
you	have	jumped
he/she/it	has	jumped
we	have	jumped
you	have	jumped
they	have	jumped

Add **ed** to the main verb.

Use the **simple present** of 'have'.

When you add **ed** to a verb, you make a **past participle**. Turn the page to find out more.

More about verbs

Present participles

To make a **present participle**, add **ing** to a verb.

fly > fly<u>ing</u>

work > work<u>ing</u>

For verbs that end in **e**, drop the **e** and add **ing**.

dance > danc<u>ing</u>
hope > hop<u>ing</u>

Some verbs **double their last letter** when you add **ing**.

stop > sto<u>pping</u>
run > ru<u>nning</u>

Past participles

To make a **past participle**, add **ed** to a verb and follow the same rules that you use for present participles.

work > work<u>ed</u>
dance > danc<u>ed</u>
stop > sto<u>pped</u>

If a verb ends in a **consonant plus y**, you need to change the **y** to **i** and then add **ed**.

carry > carr<u>ied</u>

worry > worr<u>ied</u>

bury > bur<u>ied</u>

dig > di<u>gging</u>

Irregular verbs

Irregular verbs <u>don't</u> follow the usual rules for forming the simple past and the present perfect. Here are some irregular verbs we often use.

simple present	simple past	present perfect
I do	I did	I have done
I give	I gave	I have given
I run	I ran	I have run
I dig	I dug	I have dug
I fall	I fell	I have fallen
I hide	I hid	I have hidden
I forget	I forgot	I have forgotten
I think	I thought	I have thought

Using irregular verbs

Try writing this sentence in the simple past.
(The verbs you need to use are underlined.)

Yesterday, I <u>run</u> around the lake. I <u>think</u> it would be easy, but I <u>fall</u> over and <u>give</u> myself a shock.

Now, write this sentence in the present perfect.

Sam says he has <u>forget</u> what he has <u>do</u> with my key. I <u>think</u> he has <u>dig</u> a hole and <u>hide</u> it.

Adverbs

Adverbs are words, such as 'slowly' and 'often', that work with verbs. They tell you more about the way an action is done.

The princess sang <u>loudly</u>.

| carefully | surprisingly |
| always | here | soon |

How is it done?

Many adverbs show **how** something is done. These adverbs often end in the letters **ly**.

The sun shone <u>brightly</u>.

The tiger pounced <u>suddenly</u>.

adverbs showing 'how'

Irregular adverbs

Not all adverbs that show how something is done end in **ly**. Here are some common irregular adverbs:

She played <u>well</u>.

They ran <u>fast</u>.

He aimed <u>straight</u>.

adverbs showing 'how'

When? Where? How often?

Adverbs can show **when**, **where** or **how often** an action is done.

The ice cream seller came <u>yesterday</u>.
She waited <u>outside</u> and played her tune <u>twice</u>.

adverb showing 'when'

adverb showing 'where'

adverb showing 'how often'

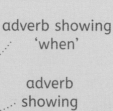

Here are some more examples:

when	where	how often
now	there	sometimes
then	everywhere	never
later	nearby	daily
tomorrow	abroad	once

Spot the adverbs

Can you spot six adverbs in these sentences?

Bertie raced inside, quickly grabbed his cape and started dancing wildly.
"I don't often complain," I said patiently, "but why do you always have to show off?"

33

Prepositions

Prepositions are words, such as 'on' and 'before', that work with nouns and pronouns. They show **where** something or someone is, or **when** something happened.

Boo skated across the rink.

These words are all **prepositions**.

across over up during
after behind in towards

next to   away from
along with   in front of

Some prepositions can be two or more words long.

Where?

Prepositions can show where something is in relation to something else.

Daisy searched for Hammy <u>under</u> the mat, <u>on</u> the shelf, <u>behind</u> the clock and <u>in</u> the teapot.

Prepositions can also show movement from one place to another.

The ducks waddled <u>through</u> the wood, <u>along</u> the path, <u>over</u> the bridge and <u>past</u> the pond.

When?

Some prepositions show when something happens.

On Tuesdays, we have an art lesson in the morning. We start at 9 o'clock and work until midday.

'Because of'

The words 'because of' act as a preposition. They help to explain **why** something happens.

Mo couldn't sleep because of the noise.

preposition

Spot the prepositions

There are seven prepositions in these sentences. Can you find them all?

Ali had his birthday party in a field on a hot day in summer. After the picnic, we sat on the grass and gazed into the distance at the lovely view.

Conjunctions

Conjunctions* are **linking words**, such as 'and', 'but' and 'because'. They provide a link between words or groups of words.

and   but   so   if
since   because
although   while

TONIGHT <u>AND</u>
TOMORROW!

Claire
<u>and</u> Claude's
magic <u>and</u>
mystery show

Linking words

Some conjunctions are used to link two words.

good <u>or</u> bad

young <u>but</u> wise

cat <u>and</u> mouse

soft <u>yet</u> strong

Linking parts of a sentence

Some conjunctions link two parts of a sentence.

first part
of sentence   conjunction

I arrived early, <u>so</u>
I could buy popcorn.

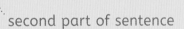

second part of sentence

These sentence parts are called **clauses**.

Go to pages 52 to 59 to find out more about **clauses**.

*Conjunctions are sometimes known as **connectives**.

Different positions

Conjunctions often go in the **middle** of a sentence, between two clauses.

We will go to the beach if the weather is good.

first clause   conjunction   second clause

You can also use a conjunction at the **start** of some sentences.

conjunction   first clause

If the weather is good, we will go to the beach.

second clause

Spot the conjunctions

Can you spot seven conjunctions in these sentences?

We were very hungry, so we ordered breakfast. The menu offered eggs and bacon or cereal and toast. The food was delicious, but we had to eat fast. Although we wanted to stay, we knew we had to rush. If we were late, we would miss our train.

Articles

Articles* make it clear which person, animal or thing you are talking about. They go in front of a noun or in front of an adjective belonging to a noun.

These are the three **articles**.

a
an
the

An explorer rowed
a boat down
the winding river.

The definite article

The word 'the' is called the **definite article**. It introduces a particular person or thing that is already known or has been mentioned before.

definite article

The explorer was astonished.

Indefinite articles

The words 'a' and 'an' are **indefinite articles**. They introduce something that is not already known.

A fly buzzed.

indefinite articles

An alligator splashed.

*Articles belong to a larger word class, called **determiners**, that includes words such as 'some' or 'those'.

38

'a' or 'an'?

If a word starts with a vowel sound (a, e, i, o or u), you use 'an' in front of it, instead of 'a'. This makes it easier to say.

The donkey ate <u>an</u> apple.

'apple' starts with a vowel, so you use 'an'

The monkey ate <u>a</u> banana.

'banana' starts with a consonant, so you use 'a'

Turn back to page 13 to find out more about **vowels** and **consonants**.

Watch out!

Some words that start with the letter **h** are used with 'an'. This is because you don't pronounce the **h** sound in these words.

I waited for <u>an</u> hour.

Carl is <u>an</u> honest boy.

Some words that begin with the letter **u** actually start with the consonant sound **y**, so you use 'a' instead of 'an'.

I'd love to meet <u>a</u> unicorn.

We're <u>a</u> united team.

Which article?

Write out these sentences using 'a', 'an' or 'the'.

I went back to __ market and bought __ pineapple, __ watermelon, __ dozen apples and __ enormous bag of cherries to make __ cherry pie. __ watermelon was delicious, but __ cherries were squishy. I had to make __ apple pie instead.

More than one word class

Some words can belong to more than one word class, depending on the job they do in a sentence.

Kylie is a good <u>cook</u>.

'cook' used
as a noun

She can <u>cook</u> very well.

'cook' used
as a verb

Maz has a <u>fast</u> car.

'fast' used as
an adjective

She drives <u>fast</u>.

'fast' used as
an adverb

Which word class?

Can you name the word class of the four words that have been underlined?

Let's have a <u>race</u> on this <u>straight</u> path.

We can <u>race</u> <u>straight</u> through the trees.

40

Spot the word class

Can you spot examples of all the
word classes in the sentences below?

- 5 nouns
- 3 pronouns
- 3 adjectives
- 5 verbs
- 3 adverbs
- 2 prepositions
- 2 conjunctions
- 2 articles

Yesterday, Josh
and I went to
an amazing fair.

We rode on the
dodgems. They
were scary but fun!

Lights flashed brightly.
Music played loudly.

Adding prefixes

You can change the meaning of some words by adding a new beginning, called a **prefix**. The word that you add to is called a **root word**.

Many **prefixes** have a meaning.

prefix + root word = new word

mid means 'middle'

<u>mid</u> + night   = midnight

inter means 'between' or 'among'

<u>inter</u> + national   = international

multi means 'many'

<u>multi</u> + coloured   = multicoloured

sub means 'under'

<u>sub</u> + way   = subway

re means 'again'

<u>re</u> + appear = reappear

super means 'above' or 'extra'

<u>super</u> + star   = superstar

Adding 'un'

When you add the prefix 'un' to a root word, you give it an opposite meaning.

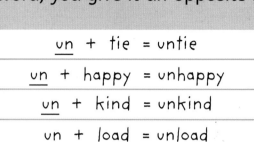

un + tie = untie	un + lock = unlock
un + happy = unhappy	un + pack = unpack
un + kind = unkind	un + wanted = unwanted
un + load = unload	un + lucky = unlucky
un + tidy = untidy	un + well = unwell

Opposite meanings

Here are some more prefixes that give an opposite meaning to a word:

dis + appear = disappear

im + possible = impossible

in + visible = invisible

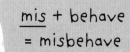

mis + behave
= misbehave

Which prefix?

Can you match these prefixes to the right root words? Write down the new words you've made.

prefixes

un   dis   re   im

root words

patient   turn
honest   fair

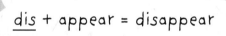

43

Adding suffixes

If you add an ending, called a **suffix,** to some root words, you can change the meaning of the word.

a care*less* cleaner

root word	+	suffix	=	new word
teach	+	<u>er</u>	=	teacher
direct	+	<u>or</u>	=	director
fit	+	<u>ness</u>	=	fitness
joy	+	<u>ful</u>	=	joyful
pain	+	<u>less</u>	=	painless
slow	+	<u>ly</u>	=	slowly

Adding 'er', 'or' and 'ness'

You can change some words into nouns by adding the suffixes 'er', 'or' or 'ness'.

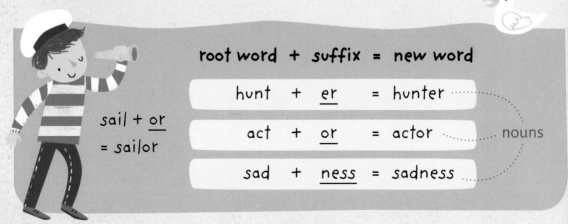

sail + <u>or</u> = sailor

root word	+	suffix	=	new word
hunt	+	<u>er</u>	=	hunter
act	+	<u>or</u>	=	actor
sad	+	<u>ness</u>	=	sadness

nouns

Adding 'ful' and 'less'

The suffixes 'ful' and 'less' can change some nouns into **adjectives** (words that give information about a noun).

noun	adjective
care + _ful_ = careful
hope + _less_ = hopeless
end + _less_ = endless

Adding 'ly'

If you add 'ly' to some adjectives, they become **adverbs** (words that give information about a verb).

adjective	adverb
quick + _ly_ = quickly
soft + _ly_ = softly
careful + _ly_ = carefully

The play_ful_ kittens purred loud_ly_.

Which suffix?

Can you match these suffixes to the right root words? Write down the new words you've made.

root word	suffix
noise collect	or ness
usual boast ill	ful less ly

45

Word families

A group of words that share the same root word is known as a **word family**.

The words in this word family are all based on the root word 'help':

helper	**help**	unhelpful
helping		helpless
helpful		helplessness
helpfully		helplessly

They need help!

This map is unhelpful.

I'm her little helper.

This word family is based on the root word 'play':

player	**play**	playgroup
playful		playtime
playfully		playground

Finding word families

Can you help the robots sort their words into word families? The four root words are on the top shelf. Find three words that are based on each root word.

act	friend	pack	appear
friendly	unpack	appearance	actor
reappear	reaction	friendship	package
repack	disappear	activity	unfriendly

Looking at sentences

A sentence is a group of words that makes sense on its own. All sentences start with a capital letter and a sentence can end with a full stop, a question mark or an exclamation mark.

WELCOME TO THE HAT SHOP!

capital letter

You look great!

We are trying on hats.

full stop

Do you like this one?

exclamation mark

question mark

TRY OUR HATS!

The Hat Shop offers headwear in a range of styles to suit all customers.

Sentences can be long or short.

Turn to pages 66 to 89 to find out more about **punctuation** in sentences.

Sentence types

A sentence can be a statement, a question, an exclamation or a command.

A **statement** states a fact or gives information. It ends with a full stop.

It is windy.

We are flying our kites.

A **question** asks something. It ends with a question mark.

Is it raining?

Have you brought an umbrella?

An **exclamation** shows surprise, disagreement, pleasure or some other strong feeling. It ends with an exclamation mark.

!

I wasn't expecting that!

I love your dress!

This is disgusting!

A **command** tells someone to do something. It can end with an exclamation mark.

!

Get down!

Go home now!

Stop barking!

More about sentences

Making sense

All sentences need at least one verb in order to make sense. It's also very important that all the words in a sentence are in the right order.

Freya a truck. ✗

     no verb

Truck drives a Freya. ✗

     words in the wrong order

Freya drives a truck. ✓

You can remind yourself about **verbs** on page 22.

Sentence fragments

Sentence fragments <u>don't</u> contain a verb, so they are <u>not</u> proper sentences. Here are some examples:

- one-word answers

Yes.　Okay.　Right.

- one-word questions

What?　Why?

- short exclamations

Hey!　Oh no!

- greetings

Hello!

Happy Birthday!

Test yourself on sentences

Look at the scene below. Can you find:

- 2 statements
- 2 questions
- 2 exclamations
- 1 command

(The punctuation marks have been left out to make it harder.)

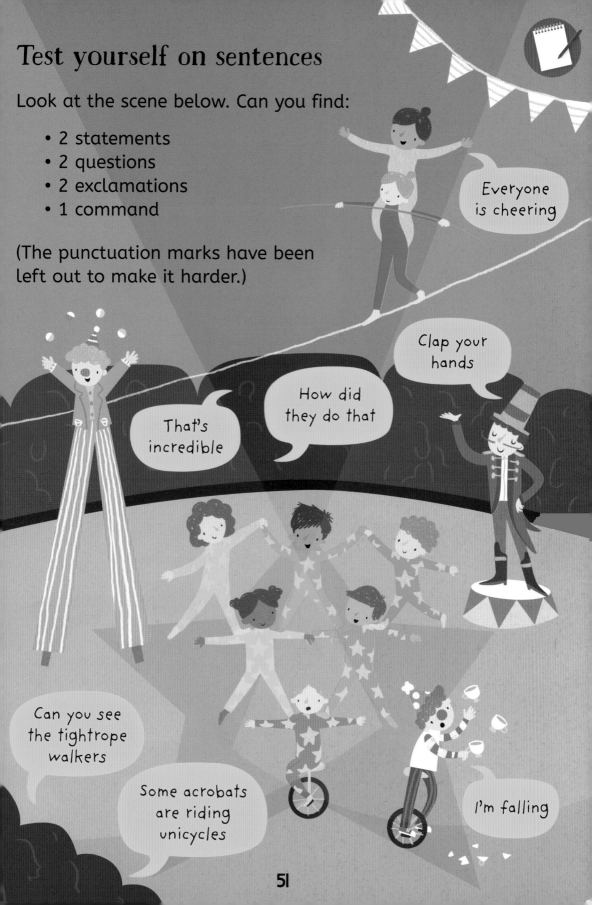

Everyone is cheering

Clap your hands

How did they do that

That's incredible

Can you see the tightrope walkers

Some acrobats are riding unicycles

I'm falling

Clauses

A clause is a group of words built around a verb. All sentences contain at least one clause.

A sentence can have just one clause.

The dragon roared.

This sentence has **one** clause built around the verb 'roared'.

Or it can have more than one clause.

This sentence has **two** clauses. One is built around 'roared' and one is built around 'shuddered'.

The dragon roared and Cuthbert shuddered.

Clauses can be short, like the examples above, or they can be long, like the ones below.

The scaly, fire-breathing dragon roared incredibly loudly and Cuthbert the cowardly knight shuddered violently.

This sentence has **two** clauses built around the verbs 'roared' and 'shuddered'.

Turn back to page 22 to remind yourself about **verbs**.

Different clauses

There are two kinds of clauses – **main** and **subordinate**. All sentences need a main clause, but only some sentences have a subordinate clause. You can learn more about main and subordinate clauses on the next few pages.

The fairy was happy.

This is a **main clause**. It makes sense on its own.

The fairy was happy because her spell had worked.

This is a **subordinate clause**. It adds information to the main clause.

Count the clauses

Can you find four clauses in this story? It doesn't matter if the clause is main or subordinate. Just remember that every verb has a clause built around it.

In the depths of the ocean, a shark circled silently. Then, it spotted some fish. It snapped its jaws and the fish scattered in all directions.

Main clauses

Main clauses make sense on their own. They are sometimes called **independent clauses**.

Some sentences have just one main clause.

Other sentences have two or more main clauses.

A spaceship landed.

main clause built around the verb 'landed'

An alien appeared.

main clause built around the verb 'appeared'

main clause built around the verb 'looked'

The alien looked around and it spotted me.

main clause built around the verb 'spotted'

Each of these sentences is made from just **one** main clause.

This sentence contains **two** main clauses linked by the word 'and'.

Linking main clauses

If a sentence has more than one main clause, the clauses are linked by the words 'and', 'but' or 'or'.

The alien stared at me
and I smiled back.

It opened its mouth,
but no sound came out.

It looked scared,
or maybe it was shy.

Each of these sentences contains **two** main clauses joined by a linking word.

Look out for the linking words below. They will help you spot when a new main clause begins.

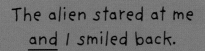

and   but   or

'and', 'but' and 'or' are all conjunctions. Turn back to page 36 to find out more about **conjunctions**.

Spot the main clauses

Can you find six main clauses and three linking words?

Do you like dogs, or do you prefer cats?
Dogs are very friendly, but they need a
lot of exercise. I take Dilly to the park
and I often play outside with her.

55

Subordinate clauses

A subordinate clause adds information to a main clause.

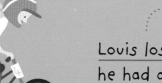

main clause

Louis lost the race because he had a puncture.

subordinate clause

These **subordinate clauses** make the main clause more interesting.

main clause

He came in last although he had trained for months.

subordinate clause

Often, a subordinate clause relies on the main clause in order to make sense.

Jet will have an accident if he doesn't slow down.

main clause

These **subordinate clauses** don't make sense without a main clause.

Kitty rides a bicycle that was designed for racing.

Introducing subordinate clauses

All the words below are used to introduce a subordinate clause. Look out for them to help you spot when a subordinate clause begins.

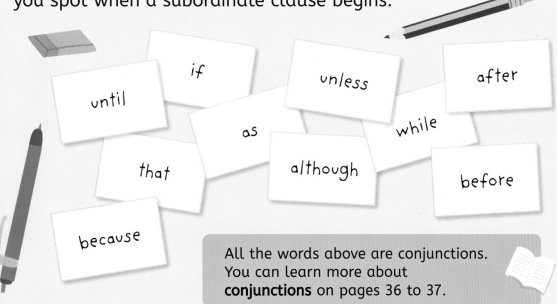

until

if

unless

after

as

while

that

although

before

because

All the words above are conjunctions. You can learn more about **conjunctions** on pages 36 to 37.

Spot the subordinate clauses

Can you spot the subordinate clause in each of these sentences?

We felt nervous before the rocket was launched.

The spaceship travelled for days until it reached the moon.

I was amazed that it could go so far.

The astronaut waved as he floated through space.

More about subordinate clauses

When a subordinate clause comes <u>after</u> the main clause, you don't need a comma to separate the clauses.

main clause comes first   no comma after the main clause

Everyone went wild <u>after</u> the music started.

subordinate clause follows the main clause

When a subordinate clause comes <u>before</u> the main clause, you need to add a comma to separate the clauses.

comma separates the two clauses

subordinate clause comes first

After the music started, everyone went wild.

main clause follows the subordinate clause

Adding commas

Each of these sentences needs a comma.
Can you work out where to put the commas?

As I left the room the parrot squawked at me.

Although we were tired we kept on walking.

If he misses his train James will be late.

Main clause or subordinate clause?

Look at the sentences below. Can you spot seven main clauses and three subordinate clauses? (Turn back to page 57 to remind yourself which conjunctions introduce a subordinate clause.)

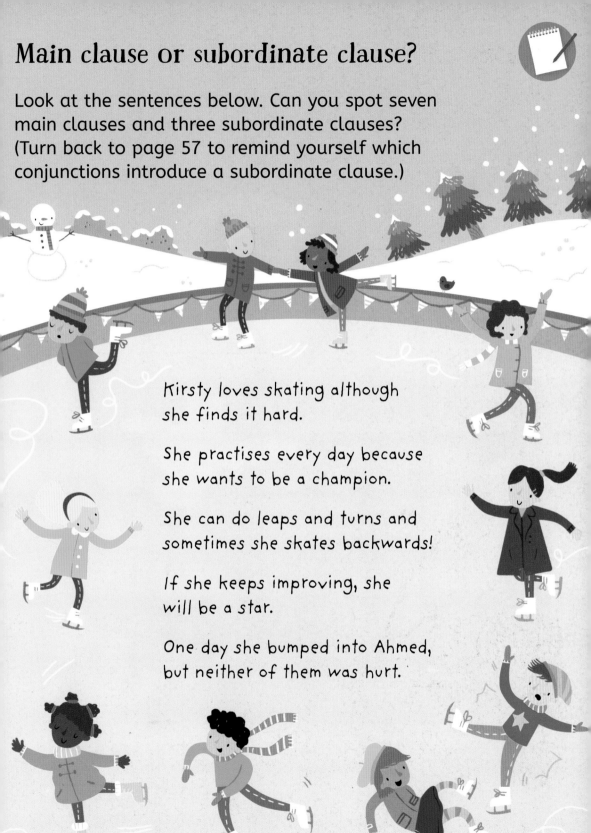

Kirsty loves skating although she finds it hard.

She practises every day because she wants to be a champion.

She can do leaps and turns and sometimes she skates backwards!

If she keeps improving, she will be a star.

One day she bumped into Ahmed, but neither of them was hurt.

Phrases

A phrase is a group of two or more words that adds extra information to a sentence. Phrases don't usually contain a verb.

Just before midnight, we reached a mansion deep in the forest. From somewhere high in the tower, a scream rang out loud and clear.

The groups of words that are underlined are all **phrases**. None of them contains a verb.

If you wrote the same sentences without any phrases, they would be much less interesting:

We reached a mansion.
A scream rang out.

Adding phrases

Can you add the right phrases to complete this story? Choose from the phrases in the green panel below.

_____, I took Trotter

for a run _____.

He chased a toddler _____

and broke a flowerpot _____.

Then he rolled _____ and barked _____.

_____, I had to take him home.

very loudly   in a rabbit suit   in the mud

in the park   In the end   Last week

with a beautiful pattern

Noun phrases

A noun phrase is a word or a group of words that adds extra information to a noun. It can be short or long.

Turn back to page 10 to remind yourself about **nouns**.

These are both **noun phrases** adding information to the noun 'plant'.

A green plant

A bright green plant with small prickly spikes.

You can use noun phrases in your writing to make it more interesting. Look at the way these sentences change:

Nancy went to the shops. She took her bag and bought vegetables, bananas and flowers.

These are **nouns**.

These are **noun phrases**.

My friendly neighbour Nancy went to the shops down the road. She took her shopping bag on wheels and bought plenty of vegetables, some lovely ripe bananas and ten pink flowers.

Spot the noun phrases

Look at the sentences on this page. Can you find six noun phrases?

In the lush green jungle, swarms of butterflies flapped their delicate wings. There were colourful flowers everywhere and some giant frogs made deep croaking noises.

Adverbials

An adverbial is a general term for a word or a group of words that adds extra information to a verb.

The penguins waddled <u>slowly</u>.

They moved <u>in an awkward way</u>.

They flapped their wings <u>as they came nearer</u>.

These are all **adverbials**.

Look how these sentences change when you add adverbials to their verbs:

The penguin <u>jumped</u>. It <u>dived</u>. It <u>swam</u>.

······ verbs ······

The penguin jumped <u>into the freezing sea</u>.
It dived <u>with a loud splash</u>.
It swam <u>smoothly and swiftly</u>.

····· adverbials

You can turn back to page 22 to remind yourself about **verbs**.

Fronted adverbials

Some adverbials can be used at the beginning of a sentence. When they go in this position, they are called **fronted adverbials**.

If an **adverbial** comes first in a sentence, it is followed by a comma.

Gradually, the clouds drifted towards us.

In the sky, a rainbow was forming.

When the storm started, we ran for shelter.

Move the adverbial

Can you rewrite these sentences to make them start with a fronted adverbial? Remember to add a comma after the adverbial.

The train set off suddenly.

It entered the tunnel a few minutes later.

We were on our way before we could wave goodbye.

Using punctuation

Punctuation is the name for a set of signs, such as commas and full stops, that are used to make writing clear. Capital letters also play an important role in punctuation.

Punctuation marks

These punctuation marks divide a piece of writing into smaller groups of words:

.	!	?	,
full stop	exclamation mark	question mark	comma

These punctuation marks do special jobs:

" " inverted commas

Inverted commas show where someone's words begin and end.

"I'm going home."

Inverted commas are also known as speech marks, quotation marks or quotes.

' apostrophe

You use an apostrophe when you put two words together. It shows where letters have been missed out.

It's snowing.

You also use an apostrophe to show that something belongs to someone.

Dad's jeans

Making sense

If a piece of writing has no punctuation,
it can be very hard to read.

where are you called shima were
in roses treehouse said lee climb
up the ladder ill help you

When you add punctuation,
you help the words
make sense.

"Where are you?" called Shima.
"We're in Rose's treehouse," said Lee.
"Climb up the ladder. I'll help you!"

Places to pause

Some punctuation marks show you
where to pause when you are reading.

Kit ate a slice of pizza,
six juicy tomatoes,
an apple and a muffin.
Then he fell asleep.

commas
showing a
short pause

full stops marking
a longer break

. Full stops

Full stops are found at the end of most sentences. They show that the sentence is finished and they mark the place where you would take a breath if you were reading aloud.

Caz took a deep breath and jumped.

full stop

Full stop, question mark or exclamation mark?

Look at pages 70 to 73 to find out more about **question marks** and **exclamation marks**.

Full stops are used **at the end of a statement** (a sentence stating a fact or giving information). Most sentences end in a full stop, but there are some exceptions.

.	It's your turn.	**Statements** end in a full stop.
?	Are you ready?	**Questions** end in a question mark.
!	I'm scared!	**Exclamations** end in an exclamation mark.
!	Jump now!	**Commands** can end in an exclamation mark, or a full stop.

Using full stops

Full stops go straight after the last word in a sentence. The full stop is followed by a single space and the next sentence starts with a capital letter.

capital letter

full stop followed by a space, then a capital letter

We found the perfect place. The beach had golden sand and graceful palm trees.

Adding full stops

The description below is missing five full stops. Can you work out where they should go? You will also need to change four lower case letters to capital letters.

Hannah watched the sun rise over the mountains the snow was sparkling the sky was blue she felt very happy it was going to be a perfect day

? Question marks

Question marks go at the end of a sentence that asks a question. They help you to recognize a question when you're reading.

Asking questions

There are three main ways of asking a question:

- Many questions start with a question word, such as 'how', 'why', 'where', 'when', 'which' or 'who'.

> Start your question with a question word.

<u>How</u> did Polly get out?

<u>Where</u> is she now?

- You can make a question by adding the verb 'do' in front of a statement.

> Use the verb 'do' to introduce your question.

<u>Do</u> you know where she's gone?

<u>Does</u> she often escape?

- You can also make a question by changing the word order in a statement so the verb comes first.

> Turn a statement around so the verb goes first.

<u>Is</u> she in the garden?

<u>Can</u> you see her?

Question tags

Another way to make a question is to add a question tag to the end of a statement. Question tags are very short questions. They are separated from the statement by a comma.

statement

Bobo's the tall one, isn't he?

comma

question tag

Using question marks

Question marks go straight after the last word in a sentence. The question mark is followed by a single space and the next sentence starts with a capital letter.

question mark followed by a single space   capital letter

Why did you squirt me? What did I do wrong?

Jojo   Bobo   Jinks   Bingo

Adding question marks

Can you add four question marks to help this passage make sense? You will also need to change four lower case letters to capital letters.

what time does the party start
do you know where it is it's not
far, is it can we go together

! Exclamation marks

Exclamation marks go at the end of a sentence that shows a strong feeling. This kind of sentence is called an **exclamation**. Exclamation marks can also be used with commands.

Exclamations

Exclamations express strong feelings, such as surprise, joy, anger, pain or fear.

I think
I've won!

I've hurt
my finger!

I'm
scared of
the dark!

She's
cheating!

Wait!

**Watch
out!**

Sit down!

Commands

Commands tell you to do something urgently.

Most **commands** are very short sentences that begin with a verb.

72

Making sentences stand out

Sometimes, writers use an exclamation mark to show that a sentence is important or surprising.

The pirate peered inside the cave. It was full of treasure!

Using exclamation marks

Exclamation marks go straight after the last word in a sentence. The exclamation mark is followed by a single space and the next sentence starts with a capital letter.

exclamation mark followed by a single space

I'm frightened! Don't leave me!

capital letter

Adding exclamation marks

The sentences below are missing four exclamation marks. Can you work out where they should go? You will also need to change two lower case letters to capital letters.

Stop right now stay where you are

This is a brilliant surprise my present is amazing

, Commas

Commas separate a word or a group of words from the rest of the sentence. They show the place where you would pause slightly if you were reading aloud.

Commas in lists

When you write a list of words, you use commas to separate them. Each word is separated by a comma, except for the last two, which are linked by the words 'and' or 'or'.

Do you prefer carrots, peas, beans or spinach?

We love apples, pears, oranges and bananas.

commas separating each thing in the list

last two items linked by 'and' or 'or'

You also use commas to separate groups of words. Look at the commas in this sentence:

We ate two apples, some delicious pears, a bunch of bananas and three oranges.

commas

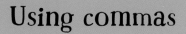

Using commas

Commas go straight after a word. They are followed by a single space and the next word starts with a lower case letter.

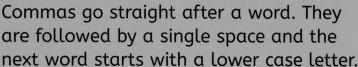

comma followed by a single space ⋯

lower case letter

The monkeys hopped, skipped and chattered.

Making things clear

Commas help to make the meaning of a sentence clear. Look at the two sentences below to see what a difference a comma can make.

Tia loves cooking her pets and her friends.

This sentence suggests that Tia loves to cook her pets and her friends!

The comma in this sentence makes the real meaning clear.

⋯ comma

Tia loves cooking, her pets and her friends.

More about commas

Commas with conjunctions

Commas often go in front of a conjunction
(or linking word) that joins two statements.

Add a comma
<u>before</u> the
conjunction.

first statement

second statement

Ben looked for the crab, <u>but</u> it had disappeared.

comma before
conjunction

conjunction

You can learn more
about **conjunctions**
on pages 36 to 37.

These conjunctions
usually have a
comma in front of
them when they
link two statements.

but
while
yet
so

Adding commas

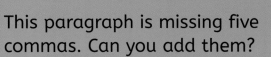

This paragraph is missing five
commas. Can you add them?

I was late so I ran to the café. I met up with Keely Ned and
Aisha. We ate pizzas a delicious salad lots of chips and some
vanilla ice cream. I had a great time but I had to leave early.

Separating statements

Some sentences have two statements that are <u>not</u> linked by a conjunction. Instead, the conjunction goes at the start of the sentence and the two statements are separated by a comma.

first statement   second statement

If it snows, we will build a snowman.

conjunction   comma between two statements

Add a comma <u>between</u> the two statements.

Look out for these conjunctions introducing two statements. Then add a comma between the two statements.

if
because
unless
although

More commas to add

Try adding one comma to each of these sentences.

Although Leo is young he is a brilliant artist.
Unless he paints every day he feels sad.
Because he is so talented he will go far.
If he keeps improving he will be a star.

More about commas

Introducing action

Some sentences start with a word or a group of words that introduces the main action. After the introduction, you need a comma to mark a pause before the action begins.

comma marks
a pause

introduction

Last week, we had a ride
in a hot-air balloon.

main action

The comma can follow a single word or a group of words.

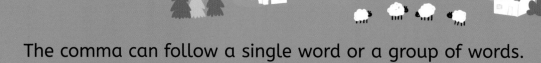

Luckily, it was sunny.

introductions
followed by
a comma

In a few minutes,
we were in the air.

When we looked down,
we saw a beautiful lake.

These introductions are known as **fronted adverbials**. Turn back to page 65 to remind yourself about them.

Adding commas and other punctuation

Look at the sentences on this page. Can you add five commas, four full stops, two question marks and two exclamation marks? (Look back at pages 68 to 78 to remind yourself how to use these punctuation marks.)

Deep beneath the waves the divers explored the reef It was amazing The coral was many shades of pink purple deep orange and blue They had seen pictures of coral before but this looked brighter Could it actually be real After they had swum around for a while they noticed the fish How had they missed them before What a fantastic experience

" " Inverted commas

You use inverted commas* to write down the words that someone says. They show where the speech begins and ends.

opening
inverted commas

closing
inverted commas

"We are learning to juggle," said Max.

Reporting clauses

When you use inverted commas, you often add a **reporting clause** to show who is speaking.

Speech that is written out like this is called **direct speech**.

"This is hard," said Ava.

These are both **reporting clauses**.

"How do you do it?" asked Erin.

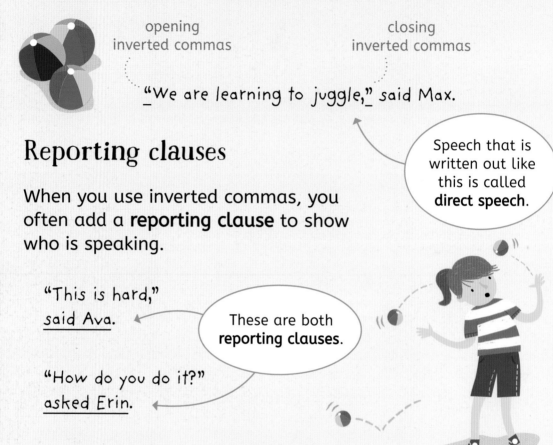

Punctuation for reporting clauses

If a reporting clause goes <u>after</u> the speech, leave a gap after the closing inverted commas. Then, start the reporting clause with a lower case letter, unless it's a person's name.

"I think I'm improving," said Max.

space and lower case letter after closing inverted commas

"You're doing well," Erin agreed.

space and capital letter for a person's name

*Inverted commas are also known as **speech marks**, **quotation marks** or **quotes**.

80

Introducing speech

When a reporting clause goes <u>before</u> the speech, it is followed by a comma and a space before the opening inverted commas.

<u>Janek said,</u> "We can juggle perfectly!"

reporting clause
introducing the speech

comma and space before
opening inverted commas

Adding inverted commas and commas

Can you add inverted commas plus one comma to each of the speeches below?

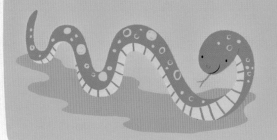

I love cats said Jack.

I prefer dogs Josie replied.

Johnny said Snakes make the best pets.

Punctuation for speech

A speech can end in a comma, a question mark, an exclamation mark or a full stop. Each time a new person speaks, you start a new line.

"This is the house," said Billy.

"Are you sure?" asked Eric.

"I'm feeling nervous!" said Lara.

Billy said, "We'll be fine."

The final punctuation mark goes <u>inside</u> the closing inverted commas.

Watch out!

Question marks and exclamation marks are usually followed by a capital letter. But when you use these punctuation marks at the end of a speech, the next word begins with a lower case letter, unless it's a person's name.

"Who's there?" <u>a</u>sked Billy.

"Boo!" <u>s</u>houted Eric.

"Stop scaring me!" Lara said.

Making statements

You use a **comma** at the end of a statement that is followed by a reporting clause.

You use a **full stop** at the end of a statement that is <u>not</u> followed by a reporting clause.

comma at end of statement

"This is the way," said <u>Billy</u>.

reporting clause <u>after</u> statement

reporting clause <u>before</u> statement

<u>Lara said</u>, "I'm right behind you."

full stop at end of statement

Spot the mistake

Each of these sentences contains one deliberate mistake. Can you write out each one correctly?

"I'm so tired!" Said Charlie.

"We're nearly there." said Maya.

"Can you see the finishing line? asked Emily.

Ivan said, "It's over there,"

' Apostrophes

Apostrophes are used for **contractions** and **possessives**. You can learn about contractions on this page. To find out about possessives, turn to pages 86 to 89.

Contractions

To make a contraction, you squash two words together and miss out one or more letters.

> **Apostrophes** show the position of one or more missing letters.

> It's amazing! I can't believe I did it!

it + is = it's

can + not = can't

Common contractions

Here are some contractions we often use. They are shortened forms of the verbs 'be' and 'have'.

be	contraction	have	contraction
I am	I'm	I have	I've
you are	you're	you have	you've
he/she/it is	he's/she's/it's	he/she/it has	he's/she's/it's
we are	we're	we have	we've
you are	you're	you have	you've
they are	they're	they have	they've

Contractions with 'not'

Some contractions are made from verbs used with 'not'.

does not	>	doesn't
has not	>	hasn't
should not	>	shouldn't
can not	>	can't

Tricky contractions

These contractions miss out a few letters or swap letters and can be tricky to spell.

I will not	>	I won't
I will	>	I'll
I would	>	I'd
I had	>	I'd

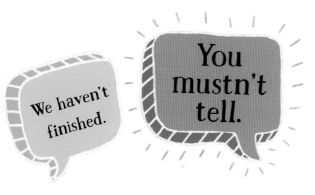

We haven't finished.

You mustn't tell.

They don't know.

He couldn't stop.

Making contractions

There are eight word pairs underlined below. Can you change them into contractions?

You have been too slow and now we are late.

It is nearly eight and our friends will not wait.

They have been waiting for hours, I am sure.

I would not be surprised if they had locked the door.

More about apostrophes

Possessives

Possessives show that something belongs to someone or something. To make a possessive, you put an apostrophe <u>after</u> the owner's name, and you usually add a letter **s**.

Oscar'<u>s</u> hat

Add an apostrophe plus 's' to show that the hat belongs to Oscar.

The cat'<u>s</u> whiskers

You can use a possessive to show that something belongs to a person, an animal or a thing.

Jake'<u>s</u> sister

The dog'<u>s</u> bone

Today'<u>s</u> weather

Charlie'<u>s</u> scarf

Watch out for 's'

If a person, animal or thing ends in a letter **s**, you usually add another **s** after the apostrophe.

The octopus'<u>s</u> tentacles

The princess'<u>s</u> tiara

The boss'<u>s</u> briefcase

The cactus'<u>s</u> spikes

The bus'<u>s</u> wheel

Names ending in 's'

If a name ends in the letter **s**, you can choose from two different spellings.

apostrophe plus 's'

Both of these spellings are correct, but you'll need to choose just one and stick to it.

Frances's flowers

apostrophe on its own

Frances' flowers

Making possessives

Can you add a missing apostrophe to each of these possessives?

Lucys boots

The walruss tusks

Last weeks news

The lionesss cubs

More about apostrophes

Plural possessives

If a noun is plural and ends in the letter **s**, you add an apostrophe on its own.

Look at pages 12 to 13 to remind yourself about **plurals**.

The boys' bedroom

The babies' toys

Ten minutes' exercise

The cats' collars

apostrophe on its own

If a noun is plural and <u>doesn't</u> end in **s**, you add an apostrophe **plus s**.

The women's shoes

The men's hats

The people's wishes

apostrophe plus 's'

The mice's cheese

Watch out!

Some people get confused between plurals and plural possessives. When they add the letter **s** to make a word plural, they add an apostrophe as well.

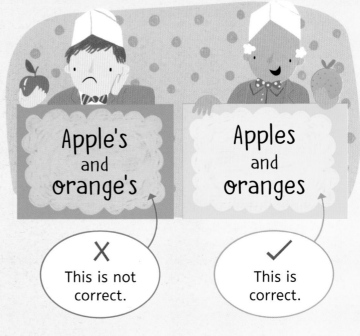

Apple's and orange's

✗ This is not correct.

Apples and oranges

✓ This is correct.

'it's' and 'its'

The little words **it's** and **its** look very similar, but they have completely different meanings.

> **it's** is a contraction of 'it is' or 'it has'.
>
> **its** is a possessive, meaning 'belonging to it'.

contraction of 'it is'

It's always great to see you.

contraction of 'it has'

It's been fun.

No apostrophe here!

Your dog has dropped its bone.

possessive

Adding apostrophes

Can you add eight apostrophes to these sentences?

Its late and the girls arent ready. All the childrens presents are missing. Lauras case has lost its handle and Lily cant find her sandals. The girls mum wont wait and theyre in trouble!

When you have added the apostrophes, count the number of contractions and the number of possessives.

Writing skills

Grammar and punctuation are very important, but there are other skills you can learn. The next few pages are filled with suggestions to help bring your writing to life.

Keep reading

I like the word 'crafty'.

The best way to learn about writing is to **read** as much as you can. Reading will help you find new ways to express yourself and will give you some great ideas to use in your writing.

I'd love to write a story about a fish.

Keep listening

If you **listen** carefully to the things people say, you'll pick up some surprising words and phrases.

Here comes a prickle-backed monster!

That's a phrase I could use...

Keep writing

You can have fun trying out different kinds of writing. Here are some ideas for you to try:

Create a diary entry for a day in the life of a grumpy robot.

Write a news report headed 'ALIENS INVADE SCHOOL'.

Tell the story of Little Red Riding Hood from the wolf's point of view.

Describe a familiar object without giving its name.

Keep a notebook

Most writers carry a notebook wherever they go. You could start your own notebook and fill it with words, phrases and ideas.

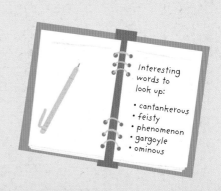

Interesting words to look up:

- cantankerous
- feisty
- phenomenon
- gargoyle
- ominous

Make it interesting!

Next time you finish a piece of writing, take a careful look at how it works. Have you chosen the best possible words, and do your sentences sound varied and exciting?

Choosing words

Some words are used so often, they no longer have much meaning. Keep a look out for overused words, such as 'nice' or 'good'. Then, try replacing them with something more interesting.

We had a <u>good</u> time at the fair. There were some <u>nice</u> rides to choose from. I had a <u>good</u> ride on a rollercoaster. It was a <u>nice</u> day.

We had a <u>fantastic</u> time at the fair. There were some <u>amazing</u> rides to choose from. I had a <u>hair-raising</u> ride on a rollercoaster. It was an <u>unforgettable</u> day.

These words make the day at the fair sound very dull.

These words bring the experience to life.

More words to try

Instead of using the same old words, why not try some of the alternatives below?

big	→ gigantic, huge, colossal, enormous, massive
small	→ little, tiny, minute, miniature, microscopic
hot	→ baking, boiling, sweltering, steamy, scorching
cold	→ icy, chilly, cool, freezing, biting, wintry

Changing sentences

If most of your sentences start in the same way, your writing will become boring to read.

When you vary the way your sentences start, your writing will immediately be more dramatic.

ROARRR!

Zak reached the cave. He felt safe at last. He heard a sudden roar. He saw a monster waiting for him.

Zak reached the cave. At last, he felt safe. Suddenly, he heard a roar. There was a monster waiting for him!

These similar sentences make the story sound boring.

These varied sentences add drama and excitement.

Glossary

abstract noun A noun that names a thing that can't be seen, heard, touched, smelled or tasted.

surprise fear courage hope

adjective A describing word that tells you more about someone or something.

silly tall yellow unusual

adverb A word that works with a verb to tell you more about the way something is done.

rudely fast never

adverbial A general term for a word or a group of words that adds information to a verb.

apostrophe A punctuation mark that shows that one or more letters have been left out, or that something belongs to someone or something.

Here's Charlie's hat

article A word that makes it clear which person, animal or thing you are talking about.

a an the

capital letter A big letter that you put at the front of a sentence, name, or place.

Sam Moscow Mrs Potts

clause A group of words built around a verb. All sentences contain at least one clause.

comma A punctuation mark that separates a word or a group of words from the rest of a sentence.

I like sausages, eggs and chips.

command A command tells somebody to do something urgently. Most commands are very short sentences that start with a verb.

Stop talking! Come here!

common noun A noun that is used to name a person, place or thing that is <u>not</u> particular. Common nouns start with a lower case letter.

banana school snake

comparative The form an adjective takes when it's used to compare two people or things.

faster taller happier

compound noun A noun made by putting two or more words together.

ice cream   motorbike

conjunction A word that makes a link between words or parts of a sentence.

and   but   because   although

consonant Any letter in the alphabet <u>except</u> for the five vowels (a, e, i, o, u).

contraction A shortened form of two words, with an apostrophe to show missing letters.

we're   isn't   can't

definite article The word 'the' is a definite article. It introduces a particular person or thing that is already known or has been mentioned before.

exclamation A sentence that expresses a strong feeling, such as surprise, fear or happiness.

I'm scared!

exclamation mark A punctuation mark that goes at the end of an exclamation or a command.

fronted adverbial An adverbial that goes at the front of a sentence, before the verb, and is followed by a comma.

full stop A punctuation mark that goes at the end of a statement.

indefinite article The words 'a' and 'an' are indefinite articles. They introduce a person or thing that is not already known.

inverted commas Punctuation marks that show where a speech begins and ends. Inverted commas are also known as speech marks or quotation marks.

lower case A lower case letter is a small letter, <u>not</u> a capital letter.

main clause A group of words built around a verb that can stand on its own.

noun A word that names a person, an animal, a thing, a place or an idea.

Annie   chocolate   Berlin

noun phrase One or more words that are built around a noun to add extra information to it.

past participle The form of a verb that usually ends in -ed.

walked   stayed   cooked

Glossary continued

past progressive Verbs in the past progressive show an action that started in the past and continued to another point in the past.

I was eating when he arrived.

phrase A group of words that adds extra information to a sentence. Phrases don't usually contain a verb.

plural More than one person or thing (the opposite of singular).

girls   foxes   parties

possessive A word showing that something belongs to someone or something.

mine   his   ours   Jake's

Binky's

prefix A group of letters added to the front of a word that can change its meaning.

uncover   return   midnight

preposition A word or words that show where something is or when something happened.

under   across   next to   in

present participle The form of a verb that ends in -ing.

walking   staying   cooking

present perfect Verbs in the present perfect show an action that started in the past and is still important now.

Josh has made a decision.

present progressive Verbs in the present progressive show an action that is happening now and continuing for a while.

Carl is eating his breakfast.

pronoun A word that can take the place of a noun.

I   me   you   she   they   us

proper noun A noun that is used to name a particular person, place or thing. Proper nouns always start with a capital letter.

Stephen   Beijing   Easter

question mark A punctuation mark that goes at the end of a sentence asking a question.

Can I help you?

reporting clause A group of words that shows who is speaking.

Jemma said   I replied

root word A word that can have a prefix or suffix added to it, in order to change its meaning.

un + <u>clear</u> = unclear

<u>clear</u> + ly = clearly

sentence A group of words that contains at least one verb and makes sense.

simple past Verbs in the simple past show an action that happened and was completed in the past.

We <u>walked</u> home.

simple present Verbs in the simple present show an action that often happens or usually happens.

Jed <u>swims</u> every morning.

singular A single person or thing (the opposite of plural).

statement A sentence that states a fact or gives a piece of information.

subordinate clause A group of words built around a verb that adds meaning to the main clause.

Sophie grinned because <u>she felt happy.</u>

suffix A group of letters added to the end of a word that can change its meaning.

sing<u>er</u> joy<u>ful</u> quick<u>ly</u>

superlative The form an adjective takes when it's used to compare three or more people or things.

fastest tallest happiest

syllable One of the blocks of sound that make up a word. (For example, the word 'won-der-ful' has three syllables.)

verb Verbs often describe an action and are known as 'doing words'. They can also be 'thinking words' or 'being words'.

run have imagine be

vowel One of the five letters: a, e, i, o or u.

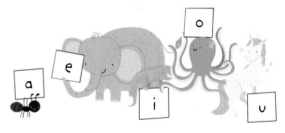

word class The name for a type of word, such as a noun or a verb.

word family A group of words that share the same root word.

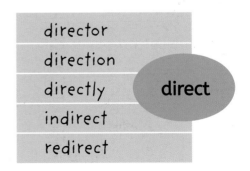

Quiz answers

Page 11
Spot the nouns:

Eva, dream, elephant, spots, bicycle, parks, Paris

Page 15
Singular to plural:

top hats, monkeys, thieves, lunches, mice, fairies, kisses, tomatoes

Page 16
Spot the pronouns:

us, him, He, it, We, I, you

Page 17
Which pronoun?

they, She, them, It

Page 18
Spot the adjectives:

calm, sunny, sparkling, proud, contented, small, green

Page 20
Making comparisons:

bigger, heavier

Page 21
Right or wrong?

The correct sentence is:

Cheese is more expensive than bread.

Page 22
Spot the verbs:

walked, swam, played, built, felt

Page 28
Present progressive to past progressive:

I was dancing. You were skipping. He was hopping. We were all having fun.

Page 31
Using irregular verbs:

ran, thought, fell, gave forgotten, done, dug, hidden

Page 33
Spot the adverbs:

inside, quickly, wildly, often, patiently, always

Page 35
Spot the prepositions:

in, on, in, After, on, into, at

Page 37
Spot the conjunctions:

so, and, or, and, but, Although, If

Page 39
Which article?

I went back to <u>the</u> market and bought <u>a</u> pineapple, <u>a</u> watermelon, <u>a</u> dozen apples and <u>an</u> enormous bag of cherries to make <u>a</u> cherry pie. <u>The</u> watermelon was delicious, but <u>the</u> cherries were squishy. I had to make <u>an</u> apple pie instead.

Page 40
Which word class?

noun, adjective, verb, adverb

Page 41
Spot the word class:

5 nouns: Josh, fair, Lights, Music, dodgems; 3 pronouns: I, We, They; 3 adjectives: amazing, scary, fun; 5 verbs: went, flashed, played, rode, were; 3 adverbs: Yesterday, brightly, loudly; 2 prepositions: to, on; 2 conjunctions: and, but; 2 articles: an, the

Page 43
Which prefix?

unfair, dishonest, return, impatient

Page 45
Which suffix?

noiseless, collector, usually, boastful, illness

Page 47
Finding word families:

act: actor, reaction, activity; friend: friendly, friendship, unfriendly; pack: unpack, package, repack; appear: appearance, reappear, disappear

Page 51
Test yourself on sentences:

2 statements: Everyone is cheering. Some acrobats are riding unicycles. 2 questions: How did they do that? Can you see the tightrope walkers? 2 exclamations: That's incredible! I'm falling! 1 command: Clap your hands!

Page 53
Count the clauses:

Clause 1: In the depths of the ocean, a shark circled silently.
Clause 2: Then, it spotted some fish.
Clause 3: It snapped its jaws
Clause 4: the fish scattered in all directions.

Page 55
Spot the main clauses:

Clause 1: Do you like dogs
Clause 2: do you prefer cats?
Clause 3: Dogs are very friendly
Clause 4: they need a lot of exercise.
Clause 5: I take Dilly to the park
Clause 6: I often play outside with her.

The three linking words are: 'or', 'but', 'and'.

Page 57
Spot the subordinate clauses:

The subordinate clauses are:

Clause 1: the rocket was launched.
Clause 2: it reached the moon.
Clause 3: it could go so far.
Clause 4: he floated through space.

Page 58
Adding commas:

As I left the room, the parrot squawked at me. Although we were tired, we kept on walking. If he misses his train, James will be late.

Quiz answers (continued)

Page 59
**Main clause or
subordinate clause?**

Main clause 1:
Kirsty loves skating
Main clause 2:
She practises every day
Main clause 3:
She can do leaps and turns
Main clause 4:
sometimes she
skates backwards!
Main clause 5:
she will be a star.
Main clause 6:
One day she bumped
into Ahmed,
Main clause 7:
neither of them was hurt.
Subordinate clause 1:
she finds it hard.
Subordinate clause 2:
she wants to be
a champion.
Subordinate clause 3:
she keeps improving,

Page 61
Adding phrases:

Last week; in the park;
in a rabbit suit; with a
beautiful pattern; in the
mud; very loudly; In the end

Page 63
Spot the noun phrases:

the lush green jungle; swarms of
butterflies; their delicate wings;
colourful flowers; some giant
frogs; deep croaking noises

Page 65
Move the adverbial:

Suddenly, the train set off.
A few minutes later, it entered
a tunnel. Before we could wave
goodbye, we were on our way.

Page 69
Adding full stops:

The full stops are underlined:

Hannah watched the sun rise
over the mountains. The snow
was sparkling. The sky was blue.
She felt very happy. It was going
to be a perfect day.

Page 71
Adding question marks:

What time does the party start?
Do you know where it is? It's not
far, is it? Can we go together?

Page 73
Adding exclamation marks:

Stop right now! Stay where
you are! This is a brilliant
surprise! My present is amazing!

Page 76
Adding commas:

I was late, so I ran to the café. I met up with Keely, Ned and Aisha. We ate pizzas, a delicious salad, lots of chips and some vanilla ice cream. I had a great time, but I had to leave early.

Page 77
More commas to add:

Although Leo is young, he is a brilliant artist. Unless he paints every day, he feels sad. Because he is so talented, he will go far. If he keeps improving, he will be a star.

Page 79
Adding commas and other punctuation:

Deep beneath the waves, the divers explored the reef. It was amazing! The coral was many shades of pink, purple, deep orange and blue. They had seen pictures of coral before, but this looked brighter. Could it actually be real? After they had swum around for a while, they noticed the fish. How had they missed them before? What a fantastic experience!

Page 81
Adding inverted commas and commas:

"I love cats," said Jack. "I prefer dogs," Josie replied. Johnny said, "Snakes make the best pets."

Page 83
Spot the mistake:

The correction in each sentence is underlined:

"I'm so tired!" said Charlie. "We're nearly there," said Maya. "Can you see the finishing line?" asked Emily. Ivan said, "It's over there."

Page 85
Making contractions:

You've, we're, It's, won't, They've, I'm, wouldn't, they'd

Page 87
Making possessives:

Lucy's boots; The walrus's tusks; Last week's news; The lioness's cubs.

Page 89
Adding apostrophes:

It's late and the girls aren't ready. All the children's presents are missing. Laura's case has lost its handle and Lily can't find her sandals. The girls' mum won't wait and they're in trouble!

There are five contractions and three possessives.

Index